Lal Batti: Cracking the UPSC Code

No Stress, Just Success – UPSC Made Easy-ish!

Lal Batti: Cracking the UPSC Code

No Stress, Just Success – UPSC Made Easy-ish!

Author: Pankaj Garg

Publisher: Notion Press

ISBN:

Printed in: India

Copyright @ 2024

Cover Photo & Design: Pankaj Garg

Dedication

To all the UPSC aspirants who have stayed awake longer than a night owl

&

To those who've stared at their books wondering if they could just Google the answers.

This book is for you – may your stress be low, your caffeine levels high, and your results even higher.

Here's to cracking the code, laughing through the myths, and making the journey just a bit more fun!

Acknowledgments

First and foremost, I want to thank my **coffee mug** *for being my silent, tireless partner in this journey. Without you, I would not have survived the countless sleepless nights filled with stacks of books and endless coffee.*

A huge shout out to all the **UPSC aspirants** *out there, who unknowingly provided endless material for this book. Your struggles, your doubts, and your questions inspired me to write something that (hopefully) makes your journey a little less stressful and a lot more fun.*

To the **mentors**, *who sometimes sounded like broken records, but hey, we all need someone to keep us on track – thank you for being the calm in the chaos (even if we didn't listen to all your advice the first time).*

This book is a product of a lot of **trial and error,** *and a few* **"I'll figure it out later"** *moments. But most of all, it's for all those who dared to take the UPSC road, despite all the myths, doubts, and occasional breakdowns along the way.*

Table of Contents

Appendices

Disclaimer

The insights, strategies, and advice provided in this book are based on my 15 years of teaching experience and my deep commitment to guiding UPSC aspirants. Although I applied for the UPSC exam, I could not reach the exam center due to financial constraints that prevented me from affording the travel expenses. Despite this setback, I have spent years mentoring and coaching students, helping them navigate the complex UPSC journey.

This book is a result of my extensive experience in coaching and supporting countless aspirants. It is written with the aim of making your UPSC preparation journey smarter, more manageable, and hopefully a bit more enjoyable. While I may not have personally sat for the exam, the strategies shared here are grounded in real-world experience and the collective learning of many successful candidates.

While this book provides guidance and practical tips, please remember that success in UPSC ultimately depends on consistent effort, smart work, and your individual dedication. This book is intended to inspire and support you, but your success will be shaped by your hard work and perseverance.

Preface

Welcome to **"Lal Batti: Cracking the UPSC Code"**, *a book that is not just about cracking an exam. It's about chasing a dream—one that might seem impossible at times, but is always worth the fight. It's about rising after setbacks, staying resilient when everything around you feels like it's falling apart, and finding strength in places you never thought to look.*

Let me tell you a story. I was once where you are now—dreaming of the day when I could wear the **Lal Batti,** *that symbol of success, after my name. I had the ambition, the fire, and the dedication. But, like so many others, life threw challenges I wasn't ready for. In my very first attempt, I was on the verge of the exam, but* **I couldn't even afford the ticket** *to get there. I didn't have the means. That was the first blow.*

*Then, due to family conditions, I had to set my dreams aside—***the dream of becoming a civil servant—***and focus on what was immediate: earning a livelihood for my family. My journey with the Lal Batti came to a screeching halt. And yet, in my heart, I refused to let go* *of the dream. I couldn't become a UPSC officer myself, but I found a new calling—helping others who were in the same boat, guiding them, pushing them towards their dreams.*

For the last **15 years,** *I've mentored countless students, helping them find their way through the chaos of UPSC preparation. I didn't have a UPSC success story to tell, but I became part of their stories—their victories, their growth, and their ultimate success. That, in a way, was my redemption.*

Now, here's the hard truth: Having a mentor can be exhausting. If you've ever had someone push you relentlessly, you know the feeling. You might even start **hating them** *for being so strict, so demanding, so relentless in their expectations. You might feel like they're asking too much, like they don't understand how hard this is.*

*But trust me—***they do.** *They understand more than you think. A mentor isn't just someone who teaches you the material—they are the ones who remind you of your potential when you can't see it. They are the ones* *who will push you to go that extra mile when you're too tired to take another step. They see the finish line, even when you're stuck in the middle of the race, gasping for breath. They push you because they know* **what you're capable of,** *even if you can't see it yourself.*

*So, when you feel frustrated, when you think your mentor is being too hard on you, take a moment. Step back and ask yourself—***why are they doing this?** *It's not to make your life harder. It's because they know what it feels like to fall, and they want to make sure you don't. They know the* **pain of failure,** *and they want you to* **avoid it.** *They know that the* **toughest roads often lead to the brightest destinations.**

This book is my way of being that mentor to you. I may not be standing beside you physically, but every word; every piece of advice here is a reflection of the guidance I've provided to my students over the years. It's written from the heart, for those who are tired, overwhelmed, and at times, ready to quit. I'm here to remind you that **your dream isn't far off.** *It's waiting for you, even when the path seems impossible.*

*So, if you ever start feeling lost, frustrated, or ready to give up, remember—*the **Lal Batti is worth it.** *And just like the mentor who keeps pushing you, don't give up when it gets tough. Keep going. Keep fighting. Your dream is closer than you think.*

Let's chase it, together.

Pankaj Garg

Introduction

The UPSC Journey (But With a Smile)

The **UPSC Civil Services Examination** *is often called the toughest exam in the country. Thousands of people try to crack it every year, dreaming of wearing that shiny civil servant badge. But here's the thing: most people don't fail because they're not smart enough. They fail because they believe in all sorts of* **crazy myths** *about the exam. Myths that make them do things that are actually more harmful than helpful.*

So, if you're reading this, you're probably one of two types of people:

1. *You're already studying for UPSC and you need some clear, honest advice to stop the confusion and frustration.*
2. *You've heard of UPSC but are just here because your friend, who's been preparing for the exam since dinosaurs roamed the Earth, told you this book will be helpful.*

Either way, welcome! Whether you've been preparing for a while or are just getting started, this is for you.

Let's be real: UPSC prep is not just about reading books. It's about surviving a **crazy rollercoaster** *of emotions, coffee binges, and constant questioning of whether you've chosen the right career. But what make it worse are* **the myths.** *The myths that keep getting passed around like some kind of magic formula. The ones that tell you to study 18 hours a day or that you need a dozen coaching classes to crack the exam. Spoiler alert:* **that's not true.**

In **"Lal Batti: Cracking the UPSC Code,"** *we're going to break down the most common myths about UPSC prep. We'll stop you from wasting time on things that don't matter, and help you focus on what really counts. Along with the myths, we'll also talk about the* **Dos and Don'ts** *of UPSC preparation. Yes, there are things you* **should** *do, and there are things you absolutely* **shouldn't** *do if you want to avoid going in circles.*

This book will help you:

- **Busting Myths:** *Get rid of all the wild ideas people have about UPSC. No, you don't need to memorize every page of the Constitution.*
- **The Dos:** *Simple, actionable tips on how to study smart, not hard.*
- **The Don'ts:** *The mistakes that can mess up your entire preparation.*
- **Pitfalls:** *The traps that even the most prepared aspirants fall into, and how to dodge them.*

*By the end of this book, you'll know what **not to do**. That's half the battle won already. UPSC might seem like a huge mountain to climb, but with the right mindset and a little humour along the way, you'll realize it's not as tough as it seems. You just need to know the right approach.*

So, grab your favorite snack (yes, snacks are a must), and let's get started on this journey. Don't worry, we'll laugh along the way, and maybe even figure out this whole UPSC thing together.

Pankaj Garg

1

The Myths of UPSC

(Busted, With a Twist of Humour)

Welcome to the **Great UPSC Myth Factory,** *where wild stories about this exam are created and shared like gossip at a family wedding. Some of these myths are so ridiculous that they'd make a Bollywood plot seem realistic. Let's grab these myths by the collar and break them down with a dose of logic—and some laughs.*

Myth 1: You Need to Study 18 Hours a Day

Ah, the classic. "Study 18 hours a day or don't even bother!" If this were true, human beings would have evolved into sleepless, coffee-powered robots by now. But let's be honest—most of us can barely stay focused for 2 hours without checking our phones.

Reality Check

UPSC doesn't reward zombies. It rewards consistency. Even 6–8 hours of **focused** *study a day is enough if you stick to a plan. Quality matters more than quantity. You could stare at a book for 18 hours and still not* *remember a thing, but an hour of focused study could be a game-changer.*

What to Do Instead

- *Plan your day realistically. Don't burn out.*

- *Take breaks. Yes, breaks are part of the plan— Netflix is not.*

- *Study smart: summarize, revise, and test yourself.*

Extra Tip: If you're studying 18 hours a day, when do you sleep? If you don't, your chances of writing "I love Maggi" in the GS paper increase drastically.

Myth 2: Coaching Classes Are a Must

People say, "Without coaching, you're like a cricketer without a bat." Coaching institutes love this myth—it's their bread and butter! They promise to make you a topper, but what they don't tell you is that the toppers were already good before they joined.

Reality Check

Coaching can be helpful, but it's not a magic wand. Most of the syllabus is self-study-friendly. What you need is a solid understanding of the basics, which you can achieve with good resources and discipline. Coaching might give you direction, but the hard work is all you.

What to Do Instead

- *Start with the NCERTs. Yes, those schoolbooks you ignored are now your best friends.*

- *Follow a structured plan. YouTube and free resources can fill in gaps.*

- *Save your money unless you really need help with a subject.*

Extra Tip: Coaching classes don't come with a guarantee. If they did, the "refund for failure" line would be longer than the coaching registration line.

Myth 3: You Must Know EVERYTHING

"Do I need to know the GDP of Madagascar or the number of trees in the Amazon rainforest?" UPSC might be tough, but it doesn't expect you to become Google. Trying to know everything will leave you overwhelmed—and probably eating your syllabus for dinner.

Reality Check

The syllabus is your guide. Stick to it. UPSC loves candidates who can **analyse and think critically,** *not walking trivia machines. Understanding concepts and connecting ideas is what matters.*

What to Do Instead

- *Focus on what's in the syllabus.*
- *Leave obscure facts to quiz shows.*

- *Practice answer writing. Nobody's asking for a Wikipedia page in your answers.*

Extra Tip: If you're spending hours memorizing dates, remember this—UPSC cares about why something happened, not just when.

Myth 4: Only English Medium Students Can Succeed

There's a popular belief that if your English isn't perfect, UPSC will reject you faster than your crush. This is completely false. UPSC doesn't discriminate based on language.

Reality Check

The exam is designed for understanding and clarity. You can write in **any language** *that you're comfortable with. What matters is how well you explain your points, not how fancy your vocabulary is.*

What to Do Instead

- *If you're confident in your regional language, use it.*
- *Improve your basic language skills if you feel they need work, but don't obsess over it.*

Extra Tip: UPSC isn't judging your grammar like your English teacher did in school. Relax.

Myth 5: You Need 10 Books for Every Subject

Some aspirants build book collections that look like they're starting a library. Let me tell you this: buying more books doesn't make you more prepared. It just makes you broke.

Reality Check

One or two standard books per subject are more than enough. The key is **revision**, *not reading new books every week.*

What to Do Instead

- *Stick to a few good books and read them multiple times.*
- *Make notes from these books for quick revision.*
- *Use current affairs for updates, not extra books.*

Extra Tip: If you're thinking of buying another book, ask yourself—"Do I even understand the ones I already have?"

Myth 6: Your Optional Subject Will Decide Everything

Choosing an optional subject can feel like choosing a life partner—you think it's the most important decision you'll ever make. But it's not.

Reality Check

The optional subject is just one part of the exam. Your overall performance matters much more. Choose a subject you enjoy or are familiar with, not one that's trending.

What to Do Instead

- *Pick a subject you're comfortable studying for months.*
- *Don't blindly follow "topper trends."*
- *Practice writing answers for your optional from the start.*

Extra Tip: Optional subjects don't have feelings. They won't be upset if you pick one over the other.

Myth 7: Mock Tests Are for the End

Some aspirants think mock tests are like dessert—you only have them after the main meal. But mock tests are more like the salt in your preparation: they're needed throughout.

Reality Check

Mock tests help you understand your strengths and weaknesses. They teach time management and show you how to approach the paper.

What to Do Instead

- *Start taking mock tests as soon as you finish a section of the syllabus.*
- *Use them to track progress, not as a final exam rehearsal.*

Extra Tip: Don't cry over low scores in mocks. They're meant to teach, not terrify.

Myth 8: You Must Clear in Your First Attempt

The pressure to clear UPSC in the first attempt is like the pressure to marry by 30—totally unnecessary. Many aspirants succeed in later attempts.

Reality Check

What matters is learning from your mistakes and improving your strategy. It's a marathon, not a sprint.

What to Do Instead

- *Focus on steady progress, not perfection.*
- *Don't compare yourself to others—everyone's journey is different.*

Extra Tip: If you don't clear in one attempt, don't worry. The world doesn't end. Keep going.

Myth 9: You Have to Sacrifice Everything

Some people think preparing for UPSC means giving up friends, family, fun, and maybe even bathing. Not true.

Reality Check

Balance is the key to success. A stressed mind doesn't learn well. Taking breaks and enjoying small moments keeps you motivated.

What to Do Instead

- *Schedule breaks in your routine.*
- *Spend time with loved ones—it's good for your mental health.*
- *Don't let UPSC take over your entire life.*

Extra Tip: Being happy makes you more productive. So yes, go out for that ice cream once in a while.

Myth 10: You Can Do It Alone—Mentors Are Overrated

Some aspirants believe they're like James Bond, tackling the UPSC mission solo. "Who needs a mentor? I've got books, YouTube, and my neighbour's cousin's notes!" But here's the harsh truth: flying solo can be risky, and without guidance, you might end up lost in the labyrinth of preparation.

Reality Check

Having an experienced mentor isn't about being spoon-fed; it's about having someone who can:

- **Keep you motivated** *on those days when you feel like throwing your notes out the window.*
- **Point out when you're off track** *(because it's easy to mistake "productive procrastination" for progress).*
- **Warn you about pitfalls** *you might not see coming, like wasting time on unnecessary resources.*

A mentor doesn't need to be a formal coach; they could be anyone with experience in UPSC—someone who knows the process and can guide you like a GPS when you're headed in the wrong direction.

Why the Myth Exists

This myth comes from the belief that mentors will spoon-feed you or that relying on someone means you're not self-sufficient. There's also the fear of blindly following bad advice, which is valid—choosing the wrong mentor can hurt more than help.

But the truth is, a **good mentor won't do your work for you.** *They'll nudge you in the right direction; tell you where you're wasting time, and help you create realistic goals.*

Extra Tip: *Think of your mentor as an alarm clock. They'll buzz when you start oversleeping (or overthinking). Sure, you can turn them off, but ignoring them might make you miss something important.*

2

The Dos of UPSC Preparation

(With a Dash of Humour)

Welcome to the land of UPSC Dos, where success is brewed with logic, effort, and a sprinkle of sanity. These are the things that work—not the "study for 18 hours while sipping tears" kind of nonsense. Let's dive into these lifesaving tips with a pinch of salt and a barrel of laughs.

1. Treat the Syllabus Like Your Crush

The UPSC syllabus is your ultimate guide. Know it inside out, like you'd know your crush's Instagram bio. Stick to it, and you'll have clarity. Ignore it, and you're in for heartbreak—also known as wasting time on irrelevant stuff.

Why It's a Must:

- *It keeps you focused.*
- *It saves you from studying random topics like "The History of Biscuits."*

How to Do It:

- *Print the syllabus and keep it everywhere: desk, bathroom, even your fridge.*
- *Check it often. UPSC doesn't ask questions outside it—mostly.*
- *Don't stray, no matter how tempting that obscure book on "Alien Economics" looks.*

2. Worship NCERTs Like Holy Scriptures

Before you jump to fat reference books that could double as gym equipment, start with NCERTs. They're simple, clear, and won't leave you questioning your life choices.

Why It's a Must:

- *They explain complex concepts without making you cry.*
- *They cover 60% of what UPSC loves to ask.*

How to Do It:

- *Read them with devotion.*
- *Don't skim; absorb them like your favorite binge-watch series.*
- *Highlight, underline, and make notes—but don't doodle. UPSC isn't asking for art.*

3. Current Affairs: Sip the Tea, Don't Drown in It

Yes, you need to stay updated, but that doesn't mean reading every headline, meme, or viral tweet. Be selective—UPSC cares about issues, not celebrity gossip.

Why It's a Must:

- *Prelims and Mains questions often have a "what's trending" vibe.*
- *Linking current events with static topics makes you sound smart.*

How to Do It:

- *Read The Hindu or Indian Express (skip the sports page unless you're aiming for a quiz show).*
- *Use monthly compilations to save time.*
- *Stop collecting newspapers like trophies. Seriously, recycle them.*

4. Answer Writing: Channel Your Inner Shakespeare (Minus the Drama)

Mains aren't just about what you know—it's about how well you write. And no, you don't need to sound like an English professor. Just be clear, logical, and concise.

Why It's a Must:

- *You're judged on structure, not Shakespearean vocabulary.*
- *Answer writing practice saves you from blank-paper panic.*

How to Do It:

- *Start small. Write answers for topics you've studied.*
- *Stick to the holy trinity: Introduction, Body, and Conclusion.*
- *Practice fitting answers within the word limit—it's an art form.*

Pro Tip: If you don't practice, you might end up writing "Water is important because it's wet." Don't be that person.

5. Revision: The Real MVP of UPSC

If studying is like cooking, revision is the salt. Forget to revise and your dish—err, exam—will taste bland. (Translation: You'll forget everything at the wrong moment.)

Why It's a Must:

- *Your brain is not a hard drive. Things disappear.*
- *Revision turns your "I think I know this" into "I know this!"*

How to Do It:

- *Revise weekly, even if it's just a quick skim.*
- *Use flashcards or mind maps—they're lifesavers.*
- *Stop re-reading the same page like it's a love letter. Move on.*

6. Mock Tests: Play Before the Big Match

Mock tests are your warm-up game. Don't wait till the end to start. They'll teach you things like time management and how to deal with tricky questions without crying.

Why It's a Must:

- *They show you your weak spots (hint: it's not always geography).*
- *They teach you how to guess smartly when you don't know the answer.*

How to Do It:

- *Take topic-wise tests early on.*
- *Progress to full-length tests when you're ready.*
- *Analyse your mistakes. Don't just stare at the score and sulk.*

7. Eat, Sleep, Move: The Holy Trinity

No, this isn't a gym slogan—it's what keeps you alive during preparation. You're not a machine. If you don't take care of yourself, UPSC won't matter because you'll be too exhausted to care.

Why It's a Must:

- *A healthy body means a sharp mind.*
- *Burnout isn't fun (unless you're roasting marshmallows).*

How to Do It:

- *Sleep 6–8 hours. Your brain needs a reboot.*
- *Eat real food, not just instant noodles. Add veggies—they won't kill you.*
- *Walk, stretch, or dance to your favorite song. Just move!*

8. Timetable: Your Blueprint for Success

Creating a timetable is easy. Following it? That's the real challenge. But trust me; having a plan keeps you from spending hours deciding what to study next.

Why It's a Must:

- *It makes you productive instead of confused.*
- *It ensures you're covering everything without panic.*

How to Do It:

- *Start with a simple weekly plan.*
- *Divide time between studying, revising, and relaxing (yes, relaxing is allowed).*
- *Don't make it so rigid that you feel like you're in boot camp.*

9. Find Your People (But Avoid Drama)

Preparing alone can feel like climbing a mountain without gear. Surround yourself with people who support you—not the ones who keep asking, "Beta, kab pass karoge?"

Why It's a Must:

- *Positive vibes keep you going on tough days.*
- *Peer discussions help clarify doubts.*

How to Do It:

- *Talk to friends, mentors, or fellow aspirants who understand the struggle.*
- *Avoid family members who only compare or complain.*

10. Fail Forward (No, It's Not the End)

Most aspirants don't clear in their first attempt—and that's okay. UPSC isn't a one-shot game. Every failure is a lesson, not a death sentence.

Why It's a Must:

- *Mistakes teach you what not to do.*
- *Perseverance is what makes you stand out.*

How to Do It:

- *Analyse your attempt honestly. Don't sugar-coat it.*
- *Improve your strategy, not just your study hours.*
- *Celebrate small wins—like completing a tough subject or acing a mock test.*

Conclusion

These **Dos** *are your ticket to sane, productive preparation. Follow them, and you'll not only prepare better but also laugh your way through the process. Remember, UPSC isn't the end of the world—it's just a glorified test. And you've got this. Let's keep going!*

3

The Don'ts of UPSC Preparation

(AKA What NOT to Do Unless You Enjoy Suffering)

If Chapter 2 was about steering your UPSC ship in the right direction, this chapter is about avoiding the icebergs that can sink it. Think of these **Don'ts** *as red flags on your path to glory—ignore them at your own risk. Or, as your future self would say, "Why didn't you just listen?"*

1. Don't Be a Resource Hoarder

"Let me just buy one more book. And another. Oh wait, here's a new test series!" STOP. *If you're collecting resources like they're Pokémon cards, you're doing it wrong. You'll end up with a library you'll never read and a headache you'll never lose.*

Why It's a Don't:

- *Too many resources = too much confusion.*
- *You'll spend more time organizing them than actually studying.*

What to Do Instead:

- *Stick to a few trusted books and sources.*
- *Treat them like your best friends—reliable, consistent, and always there for you.*

2. Don't Memorize Without Understanding

Some people think UPSC is a memory game. They try to memorize facts without context, like, "Who cares why the French Revolution happened? I just need the date!" Spoiler alert: **UPSC cares.**

Why It's a Don't:

- *Rote learning will fail you in Mains, where analysis matters.*
- *It's boring and doesn't stick.*

What to Do Instead:

- *Understand the concept first, and then learn the facts.*
- *Relate static topics to current affairs—it's like giving them a makeover.*

3. Don't Compare Yourself to Others

"Oh, they've already finished three subjects, and I'm still on page 10 of Polity!" Comparing yourself to others is a one-way ticket to stress-ville. UPSC is a marathon, not a sprint. Focus on your race.

Why It's a Don't:

- *It destroys your confidence.*
- *Everyone's journey is different—what works for them might not work for you.*

What to Do Instead:

- *Track your own progress.*
- *Celebrate your milestones, even if it's just understanding Article 368 (finally!).*

4. Don't Fall for FOMO (Fear of Missing Out)

"Hey, did you hear about that new magical course? Guaranteed selection!" There's always someone trying to sell you the next big thing. Don't fall for it. UPSC preparation is about depth, not how many new tricks you can try.

Why It's a Don't:

- *It wastes time and money.*
- *Most "magic solutions" are just rebranded common sense.*

What to Do Instead:

- *Stick to your strategy, but stay flexible for genuine improvements.*
- *Remember, consistency beats chaos every time.*

5. Don't Ignore Mains While Preparing for Prelims

A classic rookie mistake: pouring all your energy into Prelims and treating Mains like an afterthought. News flash: clearing Prelims is just the first hurdle. Mains are where the real game begins.

Why It's a Don't:

- *You'll waste valuable time after Prelims trying to start from scratch.*
- *Mains are 80% of the battle.*

What to Do Instead:

- *Start answer writing practice early (yes, even before Prelims).*
- *Cover topics that overlap between Prelims and Mains first.*

6. Don't Overdo It

"I'll study for 16 hours a day, every day!" Sounds heroic, right? Wrong. Burnout is real, and it's not fun. UPSC isn't impressed by how much coffee you drink or how little you sleep.

Why It's a Don't:

- *Exhaustion leads to mistakes and poor retention.*
- *You'll end up hating the process (and possibly yourself).*

What to Do Instead:

- *Study smart, not hard. Quality over quantity.*
- *Take breaks—your brain needs to breathe too.*

7. Don't Blindly Follow Toppers' Strategies

We get it. Toppers are inspiring. But blindly copying their strategies is like trying to fit into someone else's clothes—they're not tailored for you.

Why It's a Don't:

- *Their strengths, weaknesses, and timelines are different from yours.*
- *What worked for them might confuse you.*

What to Do Instead:

- *Learn from toppers, but customize their advice to suit your style.*
- *Experiment until you find your groove.*

8. Don't Procrastinate in the Name of "Research"

"Let me just watch one more video on the French Revolution. For context." Four hours later, you're watching cat videos and eating chips. Sound familiar? Research is good, but don't let it become your excuse for doing nothing.

Why It's a Don't:

- *You're wasting time pretending to be productive.*
- *You'll end up with half-baked knowledge.*

What to Do Instead:

- *Limit your "research" time. Set a timer if you must.*
- *Actively study—highlight, write notes, and test yourself.*

9. Don't Ignore Your Health

*"No time for exercise. I'll eat better after the exam."
Newsflash: your body doesn't care about your exam
schedule. Treat it badly, and it will fight back with
headaches, fatigue, and mood swings.*

Why It's a Don't:

- *Poor health = poor focus.*
- *Stress eating won't help you remember the
  Preamble.*

What to Do Instead:

- *Move your body—stretch, walk, or do yoga.*
- *Drink water (coffee doesn't count). Eat real
  food (chips don't count).*

10. Don't Quit Too Soon

There will be days when you'll want to give up. Maybe you didn't do well in a mock test, or someone told you UPSC is "too tough." Don't let those moments define you. Success takes time.

Why It's a Don't:

- *Many successful candidates didn't crack it on their first try.*
- *UPSC is as much about patience as it is about preparation.*

What to Do Instead:

- *Remind yourself why you started.*
- *Take breaks, not exits. Recharging is better than quitting.*

Conclusion

The UPSC journey is like walking a tightrope—you need balance, focus, and the courage to keep going. Avoid these common pitfalls, and you'll find the process not just manageable but maybe even enjoyable (okay, slightly enjoyable). Remember, success isn't about perfection; it's about persistence. Now go forth and conquer—but not before double-checking this list!

4

Common Pitfalls and How to Avoid Them

(AKA The UPSC Traps You Should Dodge)

Welcome to the chapter where we dive into the sneaky traps that aspirants fall into faster than they say, "I'll start tomorrow." These pitfalls are the reason some aspirants keep running on the UPSC hamster wheel without going anywhere. Let's decode them and learn how to sidestep them like a pro.

1. The "Tomorrow Never Comes" Trap

"I'll start with Polity tomorrow. Today, I'll just watch one YouTube video for 'inspiration.'" We all know how this ends: it's next month, and you still haven't opened Laxmikant.

Why It's a Pitfall:

- *Procrastination delays your entire schedule.*
- *It builds guilt, which makes starting even harder.*

How to Avoid It:

- *Start with anything—even five minutes of studying counts.*
- *Use timers: 25 minutes of study, 5 minutes of guilt-free scrolling.*
- *Remind yourself that "someday" isn't a day on the calendar.*

2. The "Notes Factory" Syndrome

"Why read the book when I can just make my own notes?" You start summarizing Laxmikant, and before you know it, you've written another Laxmikant. Congrats, you've reinvented the wheel—and wasted three weeks.

Why It's a Pitfall:

- *You spend more time writing than understanding.*
- *Your notes become so bloated, even you won't want to read them later.*

How to Avoid It:

- *Make concise notes. Bullet points > paragraphs.*
- *Focus on what you don't know—skip the obvious stuff.*
- *Remember, notes are a tool, not the goal.*

3. The "All or Nothing" Approach

"Either I study for 12 hours a day, or I'm not studying at all." Sounds hard-core, right? Wrong. This approach leads to burnout faster than an uncharged phone.

Why It's a Pitfall:

- *Unrealistic schedules lead to frustration.*
- *Guilt from missed goals makes you avoid studying altogether.*

How to Avoid It:

- *Set realistic, bite-sized goals.*
- *Celebrate small wins—like finishing a chapter without crying.*
- *Remember, consistency > intensity.*

4. The "Guess Game" in Prelims

"C is the most common answer, right? Let's go with C for all the tough questions." This strategy might work in a school quiz, but UPSC isn't playing around. Random guesses can sink your Prelims score.

Why It's a Pitfall:

- *Negative marking can destroy all your correct answers.*
- *Guessing wastes precious time in the exam.*

How to Avoid It:

- *Only guess when you can eliminate at least two options.*
- *Practice mocks to sharpen your decision-making skills.*
- *Remember, intuition is not a strategy—it's a backup.*

5. The "Revision? What Revision?" Mistake

"I've read everything once, so I'm good." Oh really? Wait until the exam when your brain decides to delete everything faster than a cache-clear. Revision is the glue that sticks knowledge to your brain.

Why It's a Pitfall:

- *Without revision, you forget 70% of what you learn within a week.*
- *Lack of confidence during the exam can cause panic.*

How to Avoid It:

- *Schedule weekly revisions. Yes, weekly!*
- *Use flashcards, summaries, or mind maps to make it fun.*
- *Keep revising until you can recite Laxmikant in your sleep.*

6. The "Social Butterfly" Problem

"I'm preparing for UPSC, but hey, let me attend this wedding, that party, and also go on a random trip." Balancing UPSC and your social life is tricky. Too much "networking" can leave you with no time to study.

Why It's a Pitfall:

- *You lose momentum in your preparation.*
- *FOMO (Fear of Missing Out) can spiral into guilt and anxiety.*

How to Avoid It:

- *Learn to say NO. Politely, of course.*
- *Save socializing for specific breaks—it's not an everyday thing.*
- *Remember, UPSC is a priority, not a punishment.*

7. The "Study in Isolation" Trap

*"I'll study alone because no one understands me."
Sure, but preparing alone can make you feel like Tom
Hanks in Cast Away—lonely, stressed, and talking to
imaginary friends (or your notes).*

Why It's a Pitfall:

- *You miss out on peer learning and motivation.*
- *Self-doubt creeps in when you don't discuss
  your progress.*

How to Avoid It:

- *Join a study group or online forum (but avoid
  gossip groups).*
- *Talk to mentors or fellow aspirants.*
- *Remember, even Batman has Robin.*

8. The "One Perfect Book" Fantasy

"Isn't there just one book that has everything?" Nope. UPSC is like a buffet—you need a bit of everything, not just one dish. Searching for "the one" wastes precious time.

Why It's a Pitfall:

- *You'll spend more time looking for resources than using them.*
- *No single book covers the syllabus comprehensively.*

How to Avoid It:

- *Stick to standard books for each subject.*
- *Combine books with current affairs for a full picture.*
- *Accept that perfection doesn't exist—except in your answer-writing.*

9. The "Test Anxiety" Meltdown

"I'm great at home, but in the exam hall, I blank out." This is normal—but manageable. Test anxiety happens when you haven't practiced enough under pressure.

Why It's a Pitfall:

- *Panic affects your performance.*
- *You make silly mistakes you wouldn't normally make.*

How to Avoid It:

- *Take timed mock tests to simulate the real deal.*
- *Practice mindfulness or deep breathing exercises.*
- *Go into the exam with confidence. You've got this!*

10. The "I'm Giving Up" Moment

Every UPSC aspirant hits a wall at some point. Maybe it's a tough mock test, a harsh comment, or just fatigue. The mistake? Thinking that this one moment defines your entire journey.

Why It's a Pitfall:

- *Giving up too soon robs you of a chance to succeed.*
- *UPSC is designed to test your resilience as much as your knowledge.*

How to Avoid It:

- *Take a break, not an exit. Recharge, then get back to it.*
- *Remind yourself of why you started. Visualize your end goal (and that Lal Batti car!).*
- *Seek support from mentors or friends—they've been there too.*

Conclusion

These pitfalls might seem harmless, but they can derail your preparation faster than you can say "Prelims." Avoid them with a smile, and remember: UPSC is tough, but you're tougher. Stay focused, stay consistent, and don't let these traps get in your way. Let's keep climbing—you're closer than you think!

5

The Mind Game

Building the UPSC Warrior Mind-set

If UPSC preparation were a battle, your mind would be your most powerful weapon. But here's the catch: it can also be your greatest enemy if you let doubts, distractions, or despair take over. This chapter is all about conquering the inner battlefield and turning your mind into your strongest ally.

1. The "I Can't Do This" Monster

Every aspirant has faced it—that sinking feeling of inadequacy, like you're trying to climb Mount Everest with flip-flops. But here's the truth: no one feels 100% ready. Even toppers had their "I'm doomed" days.

How to Tackle It:

- *Break the syllabus into smaller chunks. Conquer it one topic at a time.*

- *Remind yourself: If thousands before you did it, so can you.*
- *Replace "I can't" with "I will, and I'll figure it out on the way."*

2. Beware of Overthinking Overdrive

"Should I start with Polity or History? What if I pick the wrong book? What if I fail?" Overthinking is the Netflix of bad habits—it's addictive, wastes time, and doesn't leave you feeling any better.

How to Tackle It:

- *Take action instead of overanalysing. Even a small step forward beats hours of worrying.*
- *Stick to your plan. Trust the process—your effort will pay off.*
- *Treat your mind like a naughty child: gently, but firmly, tell it to stop.*

3. The Art of Dealing with Failure

Let's face it: UPSC can be brutal. Not everyone clears it on their first (or even second) attempt. But failure isn't a dead-end; it's just a speed bump on the road to success.

How to Tackle It:

- *Learn from your mistakes. Analyse what went wrong and fix it.*
- *Celebrate progress, not perfection. Even failures bring you closer to the goal.*
- *Remember, resilience is what separates the winners from the rest.*

4. Shut Down the "What Will People Say?" Radio

"Arre, Sharma ji's son became an IAS in his first attempt. What's taking you so long?" The truth is, society's expectations can be exhausting. But here's the thing—they don't write your exams, you do.

How to Tackle It:

- *Ignore the noise. People will always have opinions—don't let them live rent-free in your head.*
- *Surround yourself with positive, supportive people.*
- *Measure your success on your terms, not others'.*

5. The Myth of 24/7 Motivation

Motivation is like Wi-Fi—strong some days, non-existent on others. But guess what? You don't need to feel motivated all the time to keep going.

How to Tackle It:

- *Build discipline, not dependency on motivation. Show up even on bad days.*
- *Create a routine—your brain loves habits more than pep talks.*
- *Take small steps. Completing even one task gives you a dopamine boost.*

6. Beat the Distraction Dragon

Instagram, Netflix, random WhatsApp forwards—distractions are everywhere, lurking like villains waiting to steal your time. You'll need a solid defence to keep them at bay.

How to Tackle It:

- *Create a study environment free of distractions (bye-bye, phone!).*
- *Use productivity tools like Pomodoro timers or apps that block distractions.*
- *Remind yourself: scrolling memes won't get you the Lal Batti.*

7. Mind Your Mental Health

UPSC preparation can feel isolating, overwhelming, and downright depressing at times. But mental health isn't a luxury; it's a necessity. You can't pour from an empty cup.

How to Tackle It:

- *Take regular breaks. Burnout isn't a badge of honour.*
- *Talk it out. Share your feelings with friends, family, or a mentor.*
- *Incorporate mindfulness—whether it's meditation, journaling, or a simple gratitude list.*

8. Visualize Your Victory

If you can see it, you can achieve it. Visualization isn't just for athletes; it's a secret weapon for UPSC aspirants too. Imagine your future self-walking into the Lal Batti car. Feels good, doesn't it?

How to Use It:

- *Start your day by picturing yourself clearing the exam.*
- *Keep your goal visible—whether it's a vision board or a Post-it note on your desk.*
- *Use your dreams as fuel to push through tough days.*

9. Compete with Yourself, Not Others

Comparing yourself to others is like comparing apples to oranges—or in UPSC terms, comparing your Polity prep to someone else's Geography expertise. Everyone has their own pace.

How to Tackle It:

- *Focus on self-improvement. Ask yourself: Am I better than I was yesterday?*
- *Track your progress. Small wins add up over time.*
- *Remember, UPSC isn't a race; it's a marathon.*

10. Celebrate Small Wins

Finished a chapter? A week of consistent study? Completed your first mock test? Celebrate it! Small wins keep you motivated for the long haul.

How to Celebrate:

- *Treat yourself—chocolate, coffee, or even a small dance party at home with your siblings !!*
- *Acknowledge your progress in a journal.*
- *Share your wins with someone who understands your journey.*

Conclusion

The mind game is half the battle in UPSC preparation. By staying resilient, focused, and mentally strong, you'll not only survive the journey—you'll conquer it. Remember, the mind is a tool. Sharpen it, use it wisely, and you'll be unstoppable. Onward to the next challenge!

6

Success Strategies

What Successful Aspirants Do Right

So, no personal stories or dramatic tales of last-minute breakthroughs—let's keep it light and actionable. In this chapter, we'll break down the actual habits and strategies that successful UPSC aspirants follow. Spoiler alert: They're probably less about "magic formulas" and more about persistence, consistency, and making sure your syllabus doesn't become an elusive unicorn.

1. The Power of Planning – The Ultimate Study Schedule

Successful aspirants don't wake up and wonder, "What should I study today?" They've got a clear plan. Think of it like preparing for a big event: you wouldn't just show up without knowing what you're doing.

What They Do Right:

- **Weekly and Monthly Plans:** *Successful aspirants break their study goals into smaller, manageable tasks.*
- **Time Blocking:** *They don't let social media or random distractions steal their time. Dedicated hours for study.*
- **Flexibility:** *While a rigid plan is important, they also know when to adjust based on current affairs or new materials.*

Tip for You:
Create a study plan that's achievable—no "12 hours a day" fantasies. Make sure your brain can handle it.

2. Consistency Over Intensity – Don't Burn Out in a Week

The UPSC journey is a marathon, not a sprint. That means successful aspirants maintain consistency even on those "meh" days when they'd rather binge-watch the latest Netflix series.

What They Do Right:

- **Daily Commitment:** *They study every day (even if it's just a little), making learning a habit.*
- **Rest and Recharge:** *They know that skipping breaks can actually slow them down. Smart work > hard work.*
- **No Overload:** *They don't try to cover everything in one go. They pace themselves like a tortoise, not a hare.*

Tip for You:
Focus on building consistency. Even 2-3 hours daily is better than 12 hours one day and zero the next.

3. Embracing the Power of Revision

It's not enough to just study a topic once. The key to retaining all that information is constant revision. Successful aspirants understand that revision isn't optional—it's a part of the game.

What They Do Right:

- **Weekly Reviews:** *They revisit topics regularly. The more you revise, the more it sticks.*
- **Use of Flashcards & Mind Maps:** *These tools help quickly refresh concepts without re-reading entire books.*
- **Previous Year's Papers:** *They don't wait until the last minute. They revise old papers to understand the exam pattern.*

Tip for You:
Have a revision schedule that aligns with your study goals. Revisit topics every week until they become second nature.

4. The Role of Self-Assessment – Be Your Own Critic

Aspirants often rely on feedback from mentors or peers, but the real success comes from self-assessment. Successful candidates regularly test their knowledge and improve based on feedback.

What They Do Right:

- **Mock Tests:** *They take regular mock exams to simulate real test conditions and gauge their progress.*
- **Identify Weaknesses:** *After each test, they analyse mistakes and revisit those areas.*
- **Never Skip the Analysis:** *They don't just take the test and forget it—they look for patterns in their mistakes and correct them.*

Tip for You:

Make mock tests a regular part of your schedule and don't be afraid to fail—learn from it!

5. Managing Stress Like a Pro

UPSC preparation can be mentally taxing, and if you're not careful, stress can sabotage your progress. Successful aspirants know how to manage stress to avoid burnout.

What They Do Right:

- **Physical Activity:** *A regular workout helps clear the mind and keeps stress at bay.*
- **Mindfulness and Meditation:** *These practices help them stay grounded and focused.*
- **Relaxation Techniques:** *Taking breaks, listening to music, or even going for a walk to refresh the mind is part of their routine.*

Tip for You:
Find what helps you de-stress. Whether it's yoga, listening to music, or just taking a walk, use it to recharge your batteries.

6. Creating the Right Environment

One of the secrets of successful aspirants is that they create a productive, distraction-free study environment. Your study space has a massive impact on your focus and productivity.

What They Do Right:

- **Organized Workspace:** *They keep their desks neat and free of distractions (yes, which includes the phone!).*
- **Comfortable Yet Focused:** *A chair that supports your back and a well-lit space makes studying much more enjoyable.*
- **Routine Rituals:** *Some successful aspirants even have a pre-study ritual—like making a cup of tea or listening to a particular song—to mentally prepare for study time.*

Tip for You:

Set up a dedicated study area that's comfortable but not too cosy. Distractions should be minimal, and your study essentials should be easily accessible.

7. The Power of Mentorship – Don't Go Alone

While mentors are not magic wands, having one can seriously make your preparation smoother. They help keep you on track, give you useful feedback, and even calm you down when you think you're on the verge of a breakdown.

What They Do Right:

- **Guidance and Support:** *Successful aspirants turn to their mentors for advice, motivation, and feedback on their progress.*
- **Accountability:** *Mentors help them stay focused and avoid distractions, reminding them of the end goal.*
- **Learning from Mistakes:** *A good mentor can help you avoid the same pitfalls they faced.*

Tip for You:
If possible, find a mentor who's been through the UPSC journey. Their insights will save you a lot of time and stress.

Conclusion

While everyone's path to success is unique, these strategies are the common threads that successful UPSC aspirants weave into their preparation. It's not about finding shortcuts or cracking the code with some magical formula—it's about putting in the effort consistently, staying focused, and managing your time and mind like a pro. Success in UPSC isn't a matter of luck; it's about the right strategies and unwavering persistence.

So get ready—your path to success starts now!

7

Conclusion

The Road Ahead

Well, you've reached the end of this book, but don't think the journey ends here. In fact, what's ahead is where the real adventure begins.

Let's face it: UPSC preparation can feel like running a never-ending marathon with obstacles, confusion, and an occasional existential crisis. But here's the thing: **you can absolutely do this.** *You just need the right mind-set, the right strategies, and the determination to keep pushing through.*

Remember, UPSC is not about blindly grinding for 18 hours a day or memorizing 200-page books (unless you're a masochist—no judgment). It's about **working smarter,** *not harder.*

You will have your ups and downs. There will be days when you feel on top of the world, and days when you feel like you've forgotten how to spell "UPSC." But trust me, **every step forward counts,** *even the tiny ones.*

Dear Aspirants !!

Trust the process. It's not about taking shortcuts or trying to be someone you're not. It's about embracing the journey with all its bumps and bruises. UPSC isn't a sprint; it's a marathon. It requires patience, persistence, and a sense of humour.

Stay **consistent,** *and build habits that will take you to the finish line. But don't forget to* **enjoy the ride.** *Yes, it's stressful, but it's also a time for growth—both academically and personally.*

And remember, **success is the result of smart work,** *not just hard work. So, if you're working 12 hours a day but without a plan, well, you might end up just running in circles (and probably looking like a zombie). Instead, work strategically, plan your moves, and leave room for rest and recovery.*

Your UPSC Journey Doesn't End with the Exam – It's Just the Beginning

Once you crack the UPSC, life doesn't stop. In fact, it's just a new chapter. The Lal Batti car might be within your grasp, but it's not just the destination you've been preparing for—it's the role that follows. Whether you're shaping policy, leading teams, or making a difference in communities, this journey will change you in ways you can't even imagine.

UPSC isn't just a test—it's a transformation. A transformation that requires grit, perseverance, and sometimes, a little bit of madness. So buckle up. Your future in the Civil Services starts now.

And hey, **don't forget to laugh through the process.** *It's tough, yes, but it's also exciting, challenging, and (dare I say) even fun at times.*

Good luck! And may the Lal Batti light your way to greatness!

Appendices

A: Sample Timetable for UPSC Preparation

When you're preparing for UPSC while balancing school or college, it can feel like you're trying to juggle too many things. But don't worry, this timetable is designed for you to make the most of your time without burning out! Whether you're a college student or school-goer, it's all about managing your day efficiently and prioritizing the most important tasks.

1. Regular School/College Student Timetable for UPSC Prelims

The challenge is to prepare effectively while also keeping up with school/college studies. The key is to build a timetable that incorporates both your academic requirements and UPSC preparation. Here's a flexible plan you can adapt based on your daily routine.

Morning Session (6:00 AM – 8:00 AM)

- **6:00 AM – 6:30 AM:** Wake up, refresh (drink water, stretch, quick exercise or meditation)
- **6:30 AM – 7:00 AM:** Current Affairs (Read newspapers like *The Hindu* or *The Indian Express*)
- **7:00 AM – 8:00 AM:** Study for UPSC – General Studies Paper 1 (Indian History, Geography, or Polity)

College/School Time (8:30 AM – 3:00 PM)

- Attend your regular school or college classes. Make the most of this time to take quick notes that might be useful for UPSC (like important events or topics related to GS papers).

Afternoon Session (3:30 PM – 5:30 PM)

- **3:30 PM – 4:30 PM:** Revise notes from school/college studies (in case of exams) or focus on General Studies Paper 2 (Polity, Governance, or Current Affairs)
- **4:30 PM – 5:30 PM:** Study Optional Subject (1 hour focused study on your chosen optional subject)

Evening Session (6:00 PM – 9:00 PM)

- **6:00 PM – 7:00 PM:** Current Affairs Revision (Read through your newspaper summary or current affairs magazines like *Yojana* or *Kurukshetra*)
- **7:00 PM – 8:00 PM:** Practice Writing – Answer writing practice for UPSC, attempt previous year's questions, or work on essay writing
- **8:00 PM – 9:00 PM:** Optional Subject (If you're in college, this can be the time to focus on your major subject too)

Night Session (9:30 PM – 10:30 PM)

- **9:30 PM – 10:00 PM:** Light Revision – Quickly go through flashcards or notes from the day's study
- **10:00 PM – 10:30 PM:** Relax and get ready for bed. Sleep is essential, so don't sacrifice it for studying.

Note:

- **Weekends** can be used for full-day mock tests, revision, or additional focus on weak areas.

- On **Sundays**, relax a bit—do light revision, and focus on some self-care (or catch up on any missed work).

2. Sample Timetable for UPSC Prelims (For College/School Students with Busy Schedules)

This schedule is designed for students who have extremely busy days. It emphasizes short bursts of productive study time, using small gaps effectively.

Morning (Before School/College)

- **5:30 AM – 6:00 AM:** Wake up and refresh
- **6:00 AM – 7:00 AM:** Study General Studies (Current Affairs + Polity or History)
- **7:00 AM – 7:30 AM:** Breakfast & Quick revision of notes (read flashcards or review notes made the previous day)
- **7:30 AM – 8:00 AM:** Get ready for school/college

During College Breaks (Use Every Free Hour!)

- **10:00 AM – 11:00 AM (Break Between Classes):** Quick revision of General Studies (Geography, History)
- **12:00 PM – 1:00 PM (Lunch Break):** Answer writing practice or current affairs revision

Evening (After School/College)

- **4:00 PM – 5:00 PM:** Focused Study on Optional Subject (Try to make the most of these hours)
- **5:00 PM – 6:00 PM:** Revision of GS Paper 1 or Practice Previous Year Questions
- **6:00 PM – 7:00 PM:** Physical Exercise or Recreation (Keep yourself active and energized)
- **7:00 PM – 8:00 PM:** Revise Notes from the Day (Focus on weak areas from your school/college and UPSC)
- **8:00 PM – 9:00 PM:** Relax, Dinner

Night (Before Bed)

- **9:00 PM – 10:00 PM:** Light Study (Go through daily current affairs or watch a quick UPSC-related YouTube session)

- **10:00 PM – 10:30 PM:** Prepare for the next day's study (Organize your study material for tomorrow and set a plan)

Weekend Focus:

- **Mock Tests:** At least one full mock test every weekend (Saturday or Sunday).
- **Review & Strategy:** On Sundays, review the week's progress and adjust your strategy based on weak points.

B: Recommended Resources – Books, Websites, and More

Books

1. **General Studies (GS) Papers**
   - **History:**
     - *Spectrum's A Brief History of Modern India* by Rajiv Ahir
     - *India's Struggle for Independence* by Subhas Chandra Bose
   - **Polity:**
     - *Indian Polity* by M. Laxmikanth

- - *Introduction to the Constitution of India* by D.D. Basu
  - **Geography:**
    - *Certificate Physical and Human Geography* by G.C. Leong
    - *Geography of India* by Majid Hussain
  - **Economics:**
    - *Indian Economy* by Ramesh Singh
    - *Economic Survey* (Latest Edition by Government of India)
  - **Environment & Ecology:**
    - *Environmental Studies* by R. Rajagopalan
    - *Shankar's Environment*

2. **Optional Subjects (Depending on your choice)**
   - Refer to standard textbooks for your optional subject. For example, if you choose Anthropology:
     - *Anthropology: A New Approach* by K. P. Bhatnagar

3. **Current Affairs**

   - o **Newspapers:** The Hindu, The Indian Express, or any other well-regarded national newspaper.
   - o **Magazines:**
     - *Yojana* and *Kurukshetra*
     - *Frontline*
     - *Economic and Political Weekly (EPW)*
   - o **Monthly Compilations:** By various coaching institutes (like Vajiram & Ravi, Vision IAS)

Websites and Online Resources

1. **For Current Affairs:**
   - o PIB (Press Information Bureau)
   - o DD News (YouTube and website)
   - o Rajya Sabha TV (YouTube)

2. **UPSC Preparation Websites:**
   - o *Insights on India*
   - o *ForumIAS*
   - o *ClearIAS*
   - o *IASbaba*

3. **Government Websites:**
    - Ministry websites (especially for Environment, Polity, and Governance issues)
    - Economic Survey and Budget documents on *indiabudget.gov.in*
4. **Video Resources:**
    - *Unacademy*
    - *Byju's UPSC*
    - *Drishti IAS*

C: Strategy for Optional Subject Selection

Choosing your optional subject for UPSC is one of the most important decisions you'll make. It can make or break your preparation plan. Here's how to pick wisely:

1. **Interest and Background Knowledge**
    - **Pick something you genuinely enjoy.** If you find a subject boring, trust me, it'll show in your preparation.

- o Consider your academic background—if you have a strong base in a subject (like Geography, History, or Engineering), it may be easier to tackle.

2. **Syllabus Size and Overlap**
   - o Look at the syllabus—*is it manageable?* If it's huge, you might feel overwhelmed.
   - o Check for overlap with General Studies (e.g., if you pick Geography or Political Science, you'll find connections to GS papers).

3. **Availability of Resources**
   - o Ensure there are enough high-quality resources available for the subject—books, notes, online courses, and previous years' papers.
   - o Check whether mock tests are available for the optional subject you choose.

4. **Scoring Potential**
   - o Some subjects are known to be more scoring than others. Look at previous year's trends (although it's not a foolproof method).

o   Read up on the subject's weightage in previous exams and analyse how frequently it appears in the top scorers' choices.

5. **Time Management**

o   Don't pick a subject that requires more time than you can afford. The optional subject should complement your preparation, not overwhelm you.

o   Keep in mind that some subjects may require more time for preparation than others. Don't burn yourself out!

Tip:

A good strategy is to go through the syllabus of a few options, assess your interest level, and select the one that excites you.

With these tools and strategies, you're set for success. Make sure to pace yourself, balance your time between school/college and UPSC preparation, and remember that consistency is the key. You're not just studying to pass the UPSC exam; you're setting yourself up for a successful career.

Special Note for Gen Z Young Aspirants

Prioritize Your Goals Over Temporary Distractions

At this stage of life, you're probably balancing relationships, social media, and the irresistible urge to watch just "one more episode" of that series. There's also the endless scrolling through social media, checking the latest trends, and listening to every song that's trending. We get it—it's easy to get swept up in the excitement of it all. But if you're serious about the UPSC journey, it's time to ask yourself: Is the next episode really worth it, or is your future more important?

Here's why prioritizing your long-term goals over these short-term distractions will make all the difference:

1. *Love Can Wait (Really, It Can!) – Ah, young love. It feels like the most important thing in the world right now. But let's be real: it's probably more about feeling wanted than anything else. True love will be there when you're ready for it. Right now, the love affair you should be having is with your dreams. The relationship stuff can*

wait, and honestly, the UPSC journey is the ultimate commitment. Love will still be there when you ace the exam and have time to enjoy it!

2. *Fashion and FOMO Are Fun, But... – Fashion trends change faster than your study timetable, and FOMO (fear of missing out) will always be there. One moment you're on top of the trends, and the next, you're out of the loop. Instead of chasing fleeting fashion, why not focus on building something lasting and meaningful—like your future? UPSC is the ultimate trendsetter, and it'll never go out of style.*

3. *Social Media and Streaming Are Fun, But They Don't Build Your Future – Sure, checking out the latest meme or binge-watching shows can be fun, but think about it—how many hours do you waste scrolling through things that won't get you any closer to your dreams? The more time you spend getting lost in the digital world, the further you drift away from your goals. While it's tempting, those shows and feeds will still be there when you finish your UPSC prep.*

Let's face it: you'd rather enjoy them with the satisfaction of knowing you've worked hard, right?

4. *Entertainment as a Reward, Not a Distraction – Entertainment is great, but only when used as a reward for your hard work. You've probably heard this before, but there's wisdom in it: Netflix is for after you've cracked a tough study session, not for procrastination. A little break is fine, but it's much sweeter when you've earned it. Get your studying in first, and then reward yourself with a well-deserved break. The more focused you are now, the better your downtime will feel later.*

5. *Avoid the Mobile Trap—Stick to Keypad Phones! – Now, if you really want to step up your focus game, here's a bold suggestion: consider ditching the distractions of smartphones for a while. Use a good old-fashioned keypad phone to stay connected, but avoid the temptation of endless scrolling on apps. Trust us, the moment you start using a smartphone, it's hard to avoid the rabbit hole of*

notifications and games. A simple phone will do the job without leading you astray.

And here's the good news: You don't need to carry your entire entertainment library in your pocket. Instead, use a laptop for studying—it's more purposeful, and it will help you stay productive. Laptops are designed for work; smartphones are designed to pull you in. Go for the productivity option, and leave the distractions behind!

6. *Your Focus Now Will Set You Up for a Fabulous Future – Sure, you could spend your time watching that new series or keeping up with every trend. But in the long run, these short-term pleasures don't build anything meaningful. The UPSC journey, on the other hand, is about building a strong foundation—a future that will give you the freedom to enjoy whatever you want, guilt-free. Focus today means freedom tomorrow.*

7. *You Can Totally Do It—Believe in Yourself – You might feel like you're missing out on social*

fun or the latest trend. But guess what? The future you will be so grateful for the sacrifices you make now. You won't have to look back and say, "I wish I studied harder." Instead, you'll say, "I'm so glad I stayed focused and worked towards my dreams." And once you've cracked the exam, you'll enjoy the freedom to relax and indulge in all those distractions— without feeling guilty.

In Conclusion, we know it's hard—social media, entertainment, relationships, and all the distractions of today's world. But here's the truth: these things are temporary. Your dreams are not. The focus and effort you put in today will open up opportunities for a future that's all yours.

And remember—you can do this. With discipline, the right choices, and a little less scrolling, you'll reach your goal. Keep your eyes on the prize, and don't let anything distract you from what really matters.

So, grab that study timetable, put down the phone, and start writing your own success story. The future you is already cheering you on!

"Remember, the road to success is long and full of distractions, but with determination and focus, you'll make it to the finish line—just keep your eyes on the Lal Batti!"

Pankaj Garg

Bibliography

Chandra, Bipan. *India's Struggle for Independence*. 2nd ed., Penguin Books, 2008.

Laxmikanth, M. *Indian Polity*. 6th ed., McGraw-Hill Education, 2021.

Mishra, R. *Indian Polity for UPSC Civil Services Examination*. 6th ed., McGraw-Hill Education, 2020.

Nitin Singhania. *Indian Art and Culture for Civil Services Preliminary and Main Exams*. 3rd ed., Tata McGraw-Hill Education, 2020.

Rajaram, S. *Modern Indian History for UPSC*. 2nd ed., Tata McGraw-Hill Education, 2019.

"UPSC Civil Services Exam." *Wikipedia*, Wikimedia Foundation, 2023, https://en.wikipedia.org/wiki/UPSC_Civil_Services_Examination.

Ramesh, V. *Geography of India for UPSC Civil Services Examination*. 7th ed., Tata McGraw-Hill Education, 2021.

Singhania, Nitin. *Indian Art and Culture for UPSC Civil Services Examination*. 3rd ed., Tata McGraw-Hill Education, 2020.

Upendra Kaul. *Environment and Ecology for UPSC Prelims and Mains*. 4th ed., New Age International Publishers, 2018.

"UPSC Preparation Resources & Timetable." *InsightsIAS*, Insights Learning, 2024, https://www.insightsonindia.com/.

"UPSC Civil Services Exam Preparation Strategy." *IASbaba*, IASbaba, 2024, https://www.iasbaba.com/.

Carnegie, Dale. *How to Win Friends and Influence People*. Simon and Schuster, 1981.

Covey, Stephen R. *The 7 Habits of Highly Effective People: Powerful Lessons in Personal Change*. Free Press, 1989.

Goleman, Daniel. *Emotional Intelligence: Why It Can Matter More Than IQ*. Bantam Books, 1995.

Hill, Napoleon. *Think and Grow Rich*. The Ralston Society, 1937.

Keller, Gary, and Jay Papasan. *The One Thing: The Surprisingly Simple Truth Behind Extraordinary Results*. Bard Press, 2012.

Robbins, Tony. *Awaken the Giant Within: How to Take Immediate Control of Your Mental, Emotional, Physical and Financial Destiny!* Free Press, 1991.

Sweeney, Greg. *The 5 AM Club: Own Your Morning. Elevate Your Life*. HarperCollins, 2018.